AF487932

I Know Who I Am

by **Uwa Comfort Azubuike**

Art by **Jennifer Ledgerwood**

I Know Who I Am
Copyright © 2025 Uwa Comfort Azubuike

To request permissions, contact Uwa Comfort Azubuike at
Brunchandpray@gmail.com

Paperback: 979-8-218-81792-3
Hardback: 979-8-218-81791-6

Illustration & Layout by Jennifer Ledgerwood, www.LedgerwoodDesign.com

Published by Uwa Comfort Azubuike

This book is dedicated to my four precious
daughters- Nkemdirim, Ifeoma, Olanma, and Chizara.
Each of you carries a piece of my heart and
a light of your own.

And to my loving husband, thank you
for all your encouragement.

Introduction

This book was born when I welcomed my first daughter. In that moment, God placed these words in my heart as daily affirmations—to strengthen her, guide her, and remind her of who she is.

They became more than words. They became a declaration of faith and a constant reminder that she is destined for greatness.

In time, I felt clearly led by the Lord to share this message beyond my home. This book is the result of that calling.

It is hoped that the affirmations in this book will inspire and encourage other children to strive for greatness.

I am a child of God.

I am beautifully and wonderfully made.

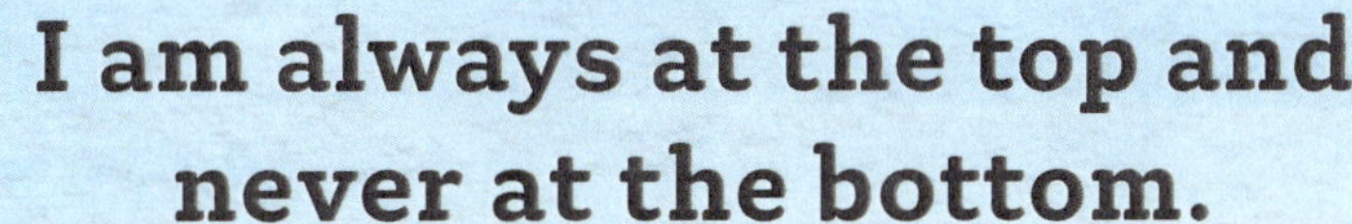

I am always at the top and
never at the bottom.

I am strong and able,
Because Jesus is behind me,
Before me and around me.

I can do ALL things through Jesus.

WELCOME
KIDS PHYSICAL THERAPY

I am not afraid
of anything

Because Jesus is with me.

Jesus loves me and He is my friend.
He cares for me all the time.

As for me
and my family,
we will serve
the Lord.

My Family

I am a leader and a follower.

I am caring and confident,
brave and strong.

I am full of wisdom, knowledge
and understanding.

I am clever, intelligent
and smart.

I will make it in life,
Because Jesus leads me.

He protects and
guides me everyday.
THE WAY

BOOK
SHOP

I will make Jesus, my parents
and my community proud.

I am always at the top
and never at the bottom.

I am beautifully and
wonderfully made.

I am a child of God.

Diploma
Dr. Nkem